HUNT A KILLER®

THE
DETECTIVE'S
PUZZLE
BOOK 2

T0203504

HUNT ◆ KILLER®

THE DETECTIVE'S PUZZLE BOOK 2

TRICKY CIPHERS,
MYSTERIOUS RIDDLES,
AND MORE TRUE CRIME-INSPIRED
LOGIC GAMES

Published by:
ULYSSES PRESS
PO Box 3440
Berkeley, CA 94703
www.ulyssespress.com

ISBN: 978-1-64604-707-9
Library of Congress Control Number: 2024934559

Printed in the United States
10 9 8 7 6 5 4 3 2 1

Writer and puzzlemaker: Liz Thompson
Project editor: Kierra Sondereker
Managing editor: Claire Chun
Editor: Renee Rutledge
Proofreader: Barbara Schultz
Interior design and layout: what!design @ whatweb.com
Shutterstock images: page 17 © BreizhAtao; page 24 © guteksk7; pages 25, 101 © Oleh Svetiukha; pages 31, 50 © Lutsina Tatiana; page 33 © Flas100; page 41 © BLKstudio; pages 54, 84, 91 © Picsfive; pages 60, 93 © TatjanaRittner; pages 67, 91 © aopsan; page 77 © ESB Professional; page 92 © VikiVecto

CONTENTS

GRAY INVESTIGATIONS

Hello,

Wow. *Hunt A Killer: The Detective's Puzzle Book 2.* I can't believe how many of you were so eager to help with my investigations that I now have the opportunity to expand this valuable training tool into a second book. I've used my years of expertise from performing my own investigations to create all-new puzzles for you to test your crime-solving skills.

Just like the first book, these pages divide the challenges into three sections of increasing difficulty. I'll start you off at Aspiring Sleuth (beginner puzzles, page 23) before promoting you to Private Investigator (intermediate puzzles, page 49) and then finally to Lead Detective (advanced puzzles, page 75). Each puzzle will offer a scenario and all the necessary hints you need to solve it.

A section at the back of the book contains all solutions to the puzzles in the order in which they appear. But to really hone your detective skills, I advise that you only review the solutions once you're absolutely certain you've already deduced the correct answer.

I'm in need of a first-rate sleuth on my team. The kind of investigator who can rise to the challenge, doesn't back down when things get hard, and possesses a curious and sharp mind.

The kind of investigator who can solve the puzzles within these pages.

I'm confident this person is you. Good luck!

Michelle Gray

Michelle Gray

INVESTIGATIVE BEST PRACTICES

Here are some tips, tricks, and strategies to keep in mind as you conduct your investigation:

1. Remember to use all of the tools at your disposal.

2. Examine every clue, sentence, or piece of evidence very carefully. You never know when an innocuous-seeming phrase will be the key to cracking a code.

3. Always keep an eye on the big picture, even when you're combing through the small details. If something isn't lining up right, try to cross-reference it with other facts.

4. Always take notes on your findings. Feel free to underline, write on, or highlight the text. Any piece of information, no matter how inconsequential it may seem at first, could prove crucial in cracking the case wide open.

CODES AND CIPHERS GUIDE

Throughout this training guide, you might come across a few codes and ciphers. People with things to hide tend to avoid leaving their secrets sitting out in the open, unprotected. I've created this list to help crack some of the most common cipher types.

ABJAD

This is less a form of cipher and more a system of writing, but I've seen it used to encode information plenty of times in the past. In simple terms, it's the omission of vowels from the text. Sometimes the writer will replace the vowels with a neutral symbol.

If you come across a word written in abjad that could be read several different ways depending on the missing vowels, try looking at the big picture. Context clues can be critical when you're trying to decipher messages written in this format.

Written in abjad, the word *example* would look like this:

- xmpl

- -x-mpl-

ATBASH CIPHER

In an atbash cipher, the alphabet is mapped onto itself backward.

Here's a chart that shows what I mean:

A	B	C	D	E	F	G	H	I	J	K	L	M
Z	Y	X	W	V	U	T	S	R	Q	P	O	N

N	O	P	Q	R	S	T	U	V	W	X	Y	Z
M	L	K	J	I	H	G	F	E	D	C	B	A

In an atbash cipher, the word *example* would be: vczmkov.

BOOK CIPHER

A book cipher needs to be used in conjunction with a pretty large section of text. This text might be found on a separate piece of paper from the code itself *or* on the same page.

The cipher tells the reader what words or letters *within* a passage to look at, and in what order, to find a hidden message.

The text can be anything from a letter to the page of a book to a shopping list, so be vigilant!

To decode a book cipher, be on the lookout for anything that might indicate on what line of a page, what word in a line, or what letter in a word you should focus.

If I wanted to call your attention to the word *example* in the following text, I could do it by providing you with the location of the word itself with this key: (2/7).

He was exacting in his standards and minimal in his praise.

He always strove to lead by example.

The key (2/7) indicates the location of the hidden word. The word *example* is on the second line. It is the seventh word of that line.

I could scatter the information even further by providing you with something like this, which gives you the necessary information in the format of **line/word/letter**:

1/1/2 1/3/2 1/6/3 1/8/1 1/11/1 2/5/1 2/7/7

H**e** was e**x**acting in his st**a**ndards and **m**inimal in his **p**raise.

He always strove to **l**ead by exampl**e**.

When read in order, the letters indicated by the key spell out the word *example*. Each set of numbers in the sequence represents the line, the word on that line, and the letter in that word.

CAESAR SHIFT CIPHER

This cipher name is based on the belief that Julius Caesar used it to encrypt his personal communications. To encode a sentence using a shift cipher, the writer shifts each letter of the alphabet forward by a certain fixed number.

For example, the top row of the following chart is the regular, un-encoded alphabet. The bottom row is the alphabet shifted forward by five letters.

A	B	C	D	E	F	G	H	I	J	K	L	M
F	G	H	I	J	K	L	M	N	O	P	Q	R

N	O	P	Q	R	S	T	U	V	W	X	Y	Z
S	T	U	V	W	X	Y	Z	A	B	C	D	E

The word *example* shifted forward by five letters is: jcfruqj.

To decode jcfruqj, you must shift each individual letter backward by five places in the alphabet.

The alphabet can be shifted by any number, although shifting by numbers greater than 26 can get a bit redundant (since, of course, the English alphabet only has 26 letters). In other words, shifting by 27 would be the same as shifting by one, shifting by 28 would be the same as shifting by two, and so on.

Remember, there are plenty of ways to add complexity to a shift cipher. Because of this, not all shift ciphers will be straight-forward. Here are a few examples of potential complications you might encounter when decoding shift ciphers:

- The shift is only used on parts of the message. Perhaps every second word is shifted, while the other words in a sentence are left alone. This can also be done by letter. For example, every third letter might be shifted, while the rest of the message is left alone.

- More than one shift is used within the same message. For example, one sentence in a message could be shifted by 12, while the next sentence is shifted by seven. On a more difficult level, this could even occur within the words themselves. Perhaps every even letter is shifted by two, while every odd letter is shifted by four.

- The shifted word itself is spelled backward or scrambled in some other manner.

- On the most difficult level, you might encounter a cipher that is layered over another cipher. In this case, you might decode a phrase into a nonsensical answer and then have to decipher it again by some additional method that is discovered in a separate place from the original key.

- To find the key to a shift cipher, look around for numbers that seem like they've been highlighted in some way or numbers that might be relevant to the cipher's writer. For example, you might find an underlined digit or a birthday. The number might be explicitly written out, or it might be hidden as part of an image or symbol. The clue might be in a painting that has 5 birds or 12 trees, telling you the shift number is 5 or 12, respectively. If you can't find a key, you can always try to "brute force" a cipher by running it through an online decryption service.

- A common variant of a Caesar shift is the date cipher. A date cipher uses a repeating number (usually a date) as the key to the shift. To encode a message with a date cipher, the numbers of the date are written above the message, with each letter being assigned one number from the date. If the message is longer than the date number, the date number is repeated as many times as necessary to reach the end of the message. For example, let's say our message to encode is "This is a date cipher." And the date to be used is December 25, 2001. The shift number is then: 12252001. So we would shift *T* by 1, *h* by 2, *i* by 2, *s* by 5, and so on. When we reach the end of the date (shifting *d* by 1), we simply start the number over again and repeat the process (shifting *a* by 1, *t* by 2, etc.) Our final encoded message is then: Ujkx ks a ebvg hkphfs. A full date is not needed to use a date cipher. It can be only a day and month, or just a year, or even a string of numbers that isn't actually a date at all but uses the same encoding process.

KEYPAD CIPHER

The basic idea of this cipher is to assign all of the letters of the alphabet to specific places on a grid like this one:

ABC	DEF	GHI
JKL	MNO	PQR
STU	VWX	YZ

While this example organizes the alphabet onto a 3x3 grid reminiscent of the keypad of a telephone, the alphabet can be spread across grids of any organization: 5x2, 3x6, and so on.

Once the writer has assigned letters to places on the grid, there must be some kind of shorthand to refer to the physical position of each letter on the grid.

Keep in mind that these grids don't necessarily have to start with *A* in the upper right-hand corner. You may need to determine how the alphabet is supposed to fall on the grid before you can start decoding.

To decode a keypad cipher, look for notes that might indicate the position of a specific letter. For example, since *A* is the first letter in the box that would be mapped onto the number *1* on a typical keypad (the model for my grid above), one way to denote its position would be 1-1. By the same logic, *E* would be 2-2, since it is the second letter in the second box.

The word *example* spelled out this way is therefore: 2-2 8-3 1-1 5-1 6-1 4-3 2-2.

PIGPEN CIPHER

A pigpen cipher is, at its core, a simple symbol substitution cipher. However, pigpen ciphers use specific geometric patterns to create a cipher. The letters of the alphabet are laid over the empty spaces of two 3x3 grids (that look like tic-tac-toe boards) and two X-shaped grids. The first 3x3 grid and X-shaped grid are empty, while the second of both grids contain dots in each empty space of the grids.

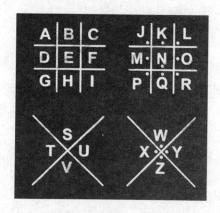

Sometimes pigpen ciphers will include the use of a keyword or phrase—whatever the "key" is, is placed at the beginning of the alphabet into the cipher—but with any repeated letters skipped. So if the phrase "Happy Birthday" was used as the key, instead of writing out the alphabet A–Z in the cipher, you would start with the letters in Happy Birthday and follow up with the rest of the letters of the alphabet making sure no letters repeat. It would look like:

H A P Y B I R T D C E F G J K L M N O Q S U V W X Z

To decode a pigpen cipher, look for any triangular or square symbols, that may or may not contain dots, in the cipher. You may need to determine how the alphabet is laid out over the geometric grids before you can begin decoding. This is what the code to a pigpen cipher would look like if the alphabet was normally laid over the grids.

A	B	C	D	E	F	G	H	I	J	K	L	M
⌐	⊔	∟	⊐	□	⊏	⌐	⊓	⌐	⌐	⊔	∟	⊐

N	O	P	Q	R	S	T	U	V	W	X	Y	Z
⊡	⊏	⌐	⊓	⌐	⌄	⟩	⟨	⌃	⌄	⟩	⟨	⌃

SYMBOL SUBSTITUTION CIPHER

A symbol substitution cipher uses symbols to represent different letters. The most common version of this cipher uses a one-to-one relationship, where one letter is represented by one symbol. To solve this type of cipher, look for short sections of symbols, usually one to three symbols long. Then try plugging in common words to see if you can determine any symbol-letter pairs are likely. This method requires a good bit of trial and error, but the code should reveal itself eventually. Sometimes keys or patterns disclose how the symbols are assigned, and if you are able to figure out that pattern, you will not have to use trial and error as much. If a unifying theme or order seems to apply to the symbols, that is a good sign that a key that can be used to make cracking the code more straightforward than simply guessing and checking.

For more information on all the previous ciphers discussed, check out these websites:

- http://practicalcryptography.com/ciphers/caesar-cipher

- https://cryptii.com

ADDITIONAL PUZZLES GUIDE

In this book you will also come across several puzzles that are not cipher related. See the list below for additional puzzle types and some accompanying information to help you solve them.

CRITICAL READING LOGIC PUZZLES

These puzzles are written as a conversation between investigators exchanging crime scene details. It's your job to pay special attention to detail and determine which facts align with which victims.

LOGIC GRID PUZZLES

Logic puzzles have several categories with an equal number of possible options for each. In order to solve the ones in this book, I've provided a grid to cross-reference the possible options in each category. Each option is used only one time. You need to determine which categories and options are linked together based on the given clues. You can eliminate pairs you know aren't possible with an *X*, and mark pairs you know are linked with an *O*. After doing this for each of the given clues, you will be able to deduce the solution to the puzzle, of which there is only one.

Example:

		MOTIVE				TIME				HOUSE COLOR			
		Annabelle	Heather	Kassidy	Tatum	8:00 a.m.	12:00 p.m.	5:00 p.m.	12:00 a.m.	Blue	Cyan	Lime	Purple
SALARY	$55,000		X		X	X				X	O	X	X
	$128,000									X	X		
	$144,000		X	X							X		
	$158,000			X							X		
HOUSE COLOR	Blue	X		X			X						
	Cyan	O	X	X	X		X						
	Lime	X	X		X	X	O	X	X				
	Purple	X			X		X						
PRESCRIPTION	Benazepril												
	Enalapril		X		X								
	Fosinopril												
	Ramipril	X											

MAZE PUZZLES

In a maze puzzle, you will follow paths through different scenarios to find an exit. Think carefully, as some mazes might have a singular rule or pattern that determines how to solve them.

SUSPECT/WITNESS PUZZLES

These puzzles provide a summary of a crime and statements made by three key witnesses or suspects. Read their testimony carefully and take notes if needed, as there may be incorrect facts or details provided that don't add up. Feel free to do some internet research if you feel stuck.

For example, say a suspect or witness claims that their alibi involved caring for their saltwater aquarium that is filled with clown fish, butterfly fish, and neon tetra fish. Some quick research will show that neon tetra fish are freshwater fish and do not go in saltwater tanks. This would expose this alibi as a lie.

WORD LADDER PUZZLES

These puzzles challenge you to morph the first word into the last word by changing only one letter at a time. Write each new word with the changed letter on each step of the ladder. Each new word must be a common English word, and the order of the letters cannot be changed. There are many ways to solve a word ladder. The provided solutions offer one way, but don't be surprised if you can figure out other words that bring you to the bottom of the ladder. Can you get to the last word before you run out of steps?

Example:

HEAD

HEAL

TEAL

TELL

TALL

TAIL

ASPIRING SLEUTH

THE DISAPPEARING DONATIONS

St. Barbara's Catholic Church has been robbed. Visiting priest Father Morgan was shocked to discover the entire weekend's donations missing from the church safe. Father Morgan was the only person spotted entering or exiting the church office, but he insists he is innocent. Besides, as a visiting priest, he has no access to the safe or knowledge of how to open it. Detectives were stumped, until a message found in Father Morgan's recently deleted texts provided the following clue. Can you determine if Father Morgan is telling the truth?

FOR RICHER OR POORER

Returning from their honeymoon at the Villa Dembo in Puertacielo, newlyweds Jason and Sara found their home had been robbed and their bank accounts cleaned out. While the bride and groom were both distraught, Sara couldn't help but wonder if the theft had anything to do with the ironclad prenup she'd had her new husband sign just before he said "I do" to joining her quite well-to-do family. And while detectives were interviewing Jason, Sara found a crumpled piece of paper that must have been left behind by the thieves. It was a letter she'd included in their wedding invitations, but with a series of dates listed on the side. Could this be a clue to determining the innocence of her new husband?

Dearest Friends,

Jason and I hope you can join us in September for an event we have all been waiting for... We're getting married! I hope you will all be able to attend. It's going to be the biggest bash our family has ever planned! (Nonna Teresa's gone a bit wild with the budget on fireworks alone!) Also, don't worry. We'll have childcare at the reception for children under five, so there are no excuses not to make it. This will be a celebration to remember for the rest of our days, take it from me!

All our love and everything, always and forever,

Jason and Sara

3/2, 4/5, 5/3, 6/4, 8/9, 10/9, 10/10, 12/5

BODY OF EVIDENCE

After defense attorney Michael Rose was discovered dead in the wet cement of a current construction dig, detectives were able to narrow their leads down to five possible suspects (his ex-wife, his current wife, a rival attorney, a former client, and a partner at his law firm) with five possible motives (protecting a secret, revenge, jealousy, money, and paranoid delusions). Detective Colby has asked you to review the notes from his suspect interviews, and mentioned he's positive that whichever suspect was motivated solely by money must have been the killer.

Can you use the following facts to pair each suspect with their motive and their relationship to the deceased, and get to the bottom of the case?

Mei-Ling, who wasn't a former client, came from an incredibly wealthy family, so she had no need for money, and she didn't have a jealous bone in her body.

Camille's potential motive was either protecting a secret or a paranoid delusion that Michael was going to try to kill her if she didn't kill him first.

Margo, who was a rival attorney, had a strong reason to want Michael dead but it wasn't for revenge.

Michael's current wife was desperate to protect a secret regarding her own illegal affairs, something that only she and Michael knew about.

Mei-Ling was Michael's partner at his law firm, and while the two were competitive, she had no paranoid delusions about her coworker.

Between Camille and Cecilia, in no particular order, one of them was passionately jealous of the attention Michael gave to others, and the other is his current wife.

Michael's ex-wife knew he still hadn't updated his will since their divorce, so she stood to inherit his entire estate if he passed away, and she desperately needed the money.

		THE MOTIVE					THE CONNECTION				
		Money	Revenge	Protect secrets	Jealousy	Paranoid delusions	Rival attorney	Current wife	Ex-wife	Former client	Law firm partner
THE SUSPECT	Phyllis										
	Cecilia										
	Mei-Ling										
	Camille										
	Margo										
THE CONNECTION	Rival attorney										
	Current wife										
	Ex-wife										
	Former client										
	Law firm partner										

SPARK OF DANGER

Change just one letter on each line to go from the top word to the bottom word. Do not change the order of the letters. You must have a common English word at each step.

FIRE

_____

_____

_____

_____

_____

_____

DEAD

DON'T WAKE THE DEAD

Richie Nguyen, the lead singer of the up-and-coming metal band Wake the Dead, was murdered last night, just before closing night of his band's first nationwide tour. The band manager found him strangled in his locked trailer at 8:05 p.m. just before he was supposed to have taken the stage with the rest of the band. Only three people had keys to Richie's trailer: Niles, the band's bassist; Maggie, his assistant; and Bruce, the band manager. After questioning all three, officers collect the following witness statements:

NILES: Richie always pre-games our shows by listening to the first album we put out. He was blasting music when I came by to check on him at 7:45 p.m., so I decided not to interrupt and ended up grabbing a beer in my own trailer instead.

MAGGIE: Richie's pretty low maintenance. He doesn't even let me disturb him at all before his shows. He says my energy is too, what's it... chaotic? But he texted me at 7:30 p.m. and asked me to bring him a new pair of headphones, like, the sound-canceling ones so he could crank his pre-show music as loud as possible without bothering the other band on the tour with us, Goat Midwinter, 'cause their trailers are right nearby. I gave him the headphones maybe 10 minutes later, and he said I could take it easy 'til after the show.

BRUCE: Sure, I found the body, but I didn't kill the guy. I stopped by to bring him a gift that Goat Midwinter sent over to thank him for keeping the music down. They'd been fighting the whole tour over Richie's noisy pre-show behavior, and I think one of them told Richie they'd give him a case of his favorite beer if he could keep it down for even one night.

After reviewing the witness statements, detectives were able to determine that one of the suspects had lied in their statement and brought them in for further questioning. Which witness was lying, and how did the detectives know?

THICKER THAN WATER

After a young woman's husband was murdered while she was out of town, all evidence pointed to a random burglary gone wrong. But when the unconvinced Detective Dubois attended the funeral, he noticed the young woman's mother behaving oddly; she almost seemed to be pleased. After obtaining a warrant for the mother's email correspondence, Detective Dubois found the following cryptic message to her daughter in her deleted sent folder, with the subject heading: TenDER HEARTS.

Can you decipher the message and crack the case?

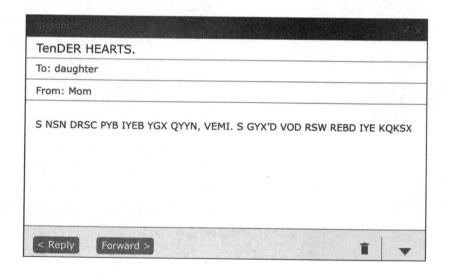

in:sent

TenDER HEARTS.

To: daughter

From: Mom

S NSN DRSC PYB IYEB YGX QYYN, VEMI. S GYX'D VOD RSW REBD IYE KQKSX

< Reply   Forward >

PAINT BY MURDER

Detective Tom West has just narrowly prevented a murder. World-renowned artist Julius Vine returned home this evening with a stolen painting worth millions, *The Wish List*, by rival artist Lira Kincaide, with the intent of destroying his rival's work. Unfortunately, serial killer Nate Blake recently became compulsively obsessed with the idea of Vine being his next victim and was waiting for Vine in his art studio upon his return. Detective West intervened just in time to save the artist's life, but unable to call for backup, he must get Blake, Vine, and the painting down the building's elevator and into his patrol car, without anyone dying or having a priceless painting destroyed.

Blake will kill Vine if left alone with him, Vine will destroy the painting if left alone with it, and Detective West must be the one to escort each person or painting in the elevator. The elevator will only fit two people or one person and one painting at a time, but Vine's art studio is small, windowless, and locks from the outside, so neither suspect would be able to escape if left behind on one of Detective West's trips. And since Detective West's trunk is full, the painting will need to be transported in the backseat of the patrol car (which cannot be opened from the inside), along with the criminals. Can you get all three men and the legendary painting to Detective West's patrol car safely?

FAMILY TIES

Bank teller Sandra Watt is the prime suspect in the robbery of her bank's local branch. Her keycard was used to enter the bank during the midnight heist, but security cameras were turned off and witnesses saw Sandra at a late-night game night, giving her an alibi past 1 a.m. The only lead detectives have turned up during a search of Sandra's home is an old-school flip phone found in her teenage son's bedroom along with half of a coded message. Can you decipher the message and see if it can help crack the case?

2-1, 6-2, 3-1

9-1, 4-3, 7-1, 3-2

9-3, 6-3, 8-2, 7-3

7-1, 7-3, 4-3, 6-2, 8-1, 7-4

6-3, 3-3, 3-3

6-1, 9-3

5-2, 3-2, 9-3, 2-3, 2-1, 7-3, 3-1

9-1, 4-2, 3-2, 6-2

9-3, 6-3, 8-2, 7-3, 3-2

3-1, 6-3, 6-2, 3-2

9-2, 6-3

6-1, 6-3, 6-1

LIES IN THE LIBRARY

This past weekend, someone posted dozens of anonymous threats on the neighborhood community app Good Fences. A digital forensics team has traced the IP of the computer being used for the posts to a local library, but there are no cameras in the library's computer lab. Luckily the timestamps of the posts overlap with the library's computer lab sign-in sheet, pointing to only three possible suspects: Alex, the librarian on duty in the lab; Noel, a high school student; and Victoria, a tenured professor at a nearby university. Detectives questioned all three suspects and collected the following statements:

ALEX: I saw both Noel and Victoria using the computer in question. I remember them because they both come to the library every weekend. Noel was pretty quiet, as always, but Victoria seemed upset, so I didn't kick her off the computer when she hit the hour limit. I didn't want to bother her, but I did notice the Good Fences app on her screen when I walked by. I left the room for two minutes to grab paper to restock the printer, and when I came back she was gone, and Noel was at the computer after her.

NOEL: My laptop broke a few months ago. During the week I use the computer lab at my school, but on the weekends I've got to come to the library to get anything done. I don't pay much attention to what other people are working on, but I remember the woman who was in the lab last weekend. She stuck out to me because she wasn't even using the computer you're asking about. The screensaver was on while she wrote in her notebook. She seemed pretty into what she was writing too. She kept laughing. It was distracting, so I was pretty glad when she finally took off after about half an hour.

VICTORIA: I've been trying to get my students more engaged in my lectures, so I started taking a class on stand-up comedy. The only problem is it's hard to find a good place to work on my material. I'm too self-conscious to write around campus, where my students could see me. And the main area of the library is so quiet, it feels too serious. I like the hum of the computer lab, so I was writing in my notebook there. I think I got some good stuff too, but there was a kid in the lab who kept shooting daggers my way whenever I laughed at a line so I only stayed in the lab for 30 minutes.

After reviewing the witness statements, detectives were able to determine that one of the suspects had lied in their statement and brought them in for further questioning. Which witness was lying, and how did the detectives know?

TAKE THE MONEY AND RUN

An accountant who handled bookkeeping for a number of wealthy VIPs has fled town after rumors spread that he'd embezzled millions from his trusting clients. He wasn't able to empty out his personal safe before fleeing though, and detectives hope getting into the safe will give them the evidence they need to confirm the whispers about his less-than-legal activities.

The safe itself is uncrackable without a code, but a series of math equations found taped to the bottom of the safe look like they could provide the numbers needed to open the safe.

Can you find the correct path through the maze from start to finish by solving the equations required in the direction you want to move? Start at 10 and end at 100. You may only travel down or to the right, but the answers you find along the correct path from 10 to 100 will provide you with the numbers needed in order to unlock the safe!

(10) ÷ 5 $(\quad)$ x 27 $(\quad)$ + 41 $(\quad)$

+ 17   + 11   - 23   ÷ 5

$(\quad)$ x 3 $(\quad)$ - 53 $(\quad)$ + 60 $(\quad)$

÷ 3   - 37   ÷ 2   x 4

$(\quad)$ - 1 $(\quad)$ x 2 $(\quad)$ - 13 $(\quad)$

+ 31   ÷ 4   x 7   + 9

$(\quad)$ x 2 $(\quad)$ - 14 $(\quad)$ + 2 (100)

OUT OF LINE

The police have caught notorious jewel thief Benny Crews, but in order to put him away for good, a witness will need to positively identify Benny, picking him out of a lineup made up of a number of well-known law breakers. After the lineup was completed, officers realized they hadn't written down the order the criminals stood in the lineup, and had to re-create the order from memory. The officers involved were positive of the following:

If Benny stood in position 5, then either Redd or Carver was in position 4.

Cord stood to the left of Redd.

Carver stood to the right of Tommy.

Benny was directly next to Cord.

Pete stood to the left of Tommy.

And Carver was in position 3.

Whoever was in position 4 was positively identified by the witness as the guilty party. What order did the criminals stand in, and was Benny the ID'd suspect?

DON'T LET HIM FIND YOU

Change just one letter on each line to go from the top word to the bottom word. Do not change the order of the letters. You must have a common English word at each step.

L I S T E N

_____

_____

_____

_____

_____

K I L L E R

'TIL WHOSE DEATH DO WE PART

A body was found this morning in Lake Michigan and was later identified as a groomsman named Jack who had gone missing from a wedding reception held on a yacht the night before. Security footage showed Jack and the groom heading toward the bow of the ship. Fifteen minutes later it showed the groom returning alone, but no cameras were able to capture what happened in between. The groom claims Jack asked to be alone, but a few wedding guests say the groom had been upset all night ever since he saw a now-deleted text message on his new wife's phone. While the bride's phone has disappeared, officers used her laptop to uncover the missing synced text—what appears to be a coded message she sent to a burner phone along with a photo of a car shifted into reverse. Can you decode the message and uncover any possible motive for foul play?

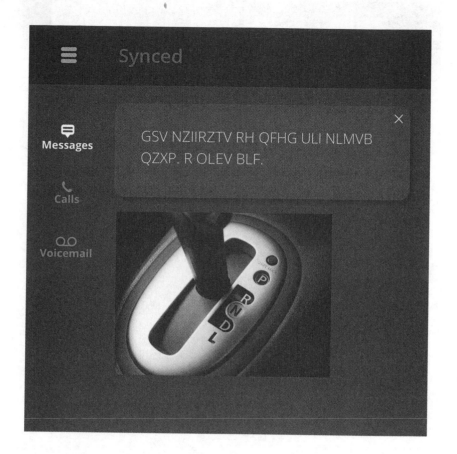

Synced

Messages

GSV NZIIRZTV RH QFHG ULI NLMVB QZXP. R OLEV BLF.

✕

Calls

Voicemail

THE HONORABLE DETECTIVES

Five detectives are being celebrated this evening at the Royal Tree Banquet Hall in Three Pines, Colorado. Each detective (Blake, Orsen, Campos, Franklin, and Torres) will receive an award for outstanding work in their field in honor of the cases they cracked that made their careers. Can you pair the detective with the type of case that made them famous (bank robbery, murder, arson, narcotics, and cybercrime) and the year they joined the police force?

The detective who foiled an infamous bank robber has been an officer longer than any of the other award recipients.

Orsen joined the force a year before Campos but a year after Blake.

The detective who busted a drug ring joined the force the year after the person who brought down a serial arsonist.

The person who solved a murder that caught nationwide attention became a police officer in 2010.

Out of the five detectives, Campos hasn't been on the force for the longest or the shortest periods of time.

Torres became a household name in his home state after solving one particular case, but it wasn't a bank robbery, a narcotics bust, or a case that involved fire.

Franklin joined the police force in 2012 and has never handled an arson case.

	CAREER-MAKING CASES					JOINED THE FORCE				
	Bank Robbery	Arson	Cybercrime	Narcotics	Murder	2009	2010	2011	2012	2013
DETECTIVE Campos										
Blake										
Orsen										
Franklin										
Torres										
JOINED THE FORCE 2009										
2010										
2011										
2012										
2013										

A MOROSE CODE

Over the last few weeks, a number of bodies have turned up in the Pershing River. At first, the police thought the deaths were accidental, perhaps the result of drunk pedestrians wandering alone too close to the edge of the water. But a medical examiner noticed that a few of the most recent victims all had the same fresh tattoo on their backs. Detective Calhaney recognized the symbols from his time serving in the Air Force, and believes the tattoo could be the key to figuring out if these deaths are the work of local organized crime, related to a local drug ring run by a dealer known as The Bank, or the work of a yet-to-be-determined serial killer. Can you crack the code faster than Calhaney?

RISING STARS

Detectives Conner, Logan, and Harold have made a splash by playing a crucial role in cracking some big cases and being promoted to detective, all before the age of 30. The detectives cracked their big cases in the same year, but their ages were only one to two years apart from one another.

When Detective Conner solved his first case, he was older than the detective was whose first big case brought down a Ponzi schemer.

The Detective who took down the tax evader was the oldest of the three when he cracked his first case at the age of 27.

Detective Logan didn't arrest the Ponzi schemer or the political blackmailer.

Which detective arrested which criminal, and how old was the youngest of them when he solved his first big case?

PICK YOUR POISON

A notorious game-obsessed killer has trapped you in a room with three buttons to choose from and a single maze as your only possible key to escape. Press the right button, and the door barring your way to freedom will be unlocked. Press either of the wrong buttons, or delay making a choice for longer than 90 seconds, and a poisonous gas will be released into the room, killing you within moments. But, solve the twisted maze left behind by the twisted killer, and it will point you to the correct button to push and lead you to your freedom. Can you find the right path before your time runs out?

PRIVATE
INVESTIGATOR

M.I.A. OR R.I.P.

Senator Viola Martin has gone missing three days after declaring her run for president. Her passport, wallet, and a few personal items have also disappeared, but the police think there's more to her disappearance than just a desire to get away. A search of her home and office turned up nothing, but Detective Arlen thinks the last email she opened on her laptop on February 19, the day she disappeared, might hold the key to unraveling this mystery. Can you crack this cryptic correspondence and find out what happened to the senator?

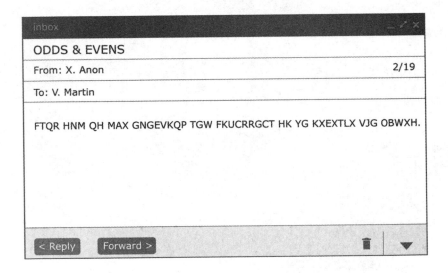

> **inbox**
>
> ## ODDS & EVENS
>
> From: X. Anon   2/19
>
> To: V. Martin
>
> FTQR HNM QH MAX GNGEVKQP TGW FKUCRRGCT HK YG KXEXTLX VJG OBWXH.
>
> < Reply   Forward >

BAD BLOOD

Retired police detective Brendan Pierce is writing a book about one of the oddest murder cases he handled over the course of his 45 years serving the town of Tall Oaks, Ohio. In a weird twist of events, five inheritance-seeking family members killed one another after the death of their family's matriarch left them with tens of millions in cash to split, with each suspect taking out another in a different way. Can you help Pierce organize his notes regarding the case by pairing the occupation of the killer with their weapon of choice, their relationship to the deceased matriarch, and what order they were killed?

One of the women used a gun in their murder, rigging it to go off at a certain time, and the other was a bartender at local pub Bar None.

The mayor, who was killed first, was not the son who killed a relative in a hit and run.

The husband died earlier than the murderer who used poison, and the poisoner was not killed last.

The killer who died 4th was murdered shortly after sprinkling a bag of crushed peanut dust into the smoothie of their victim, who happened to have a severe peanut allergy.

The murderer who used a pillow to smother their victim to death was a much-adored news anchor at KNW5 before becoming the news themselves.

The granddaughter was killed later than the tattoo artist who had made a name for themselves at Stamp Tramp's Tattoos.

		News Anchor	Bartender	Mayor	English Teacher	Tattoo Artist
RELATIONSHIP	Sister					
	Son					
	Nephew					
	Husband					
	Granddaughter					
ORDER OF DEATH	1st					
	2nd					
	3rd					
	4th					
	5th					
WEAPON	Gun					
	Pillow					
	Car					
	Peanuts					
	Poison					

OCCUPATION

WEAPON					ORDER OF DEATH				
Gun	Pillow	Car	Peanuts	Poison	1st	2nd	3rd	4th	5th

When Jane Kennicut was found not guilty of killing her millionaire husband despite the mountains of evidence against her, even her own attorney was shocked by the verdict. After an anonymous tip came in claiming the jury had been tampered with, a thorough search was done of the hotel rooms where the jury members had been sequestered. Unfortunately, eight of the rooms had already been cleaned by the hotel staff, but of the remaining four rooms, three contained empty red envelopes in the trash, and the fourth contained a red envelope and a note inside that looked like it was written in some kind of code. Can you decipher this lone piece of evidence and make sure justice is served?

URUGB GSLFHZMW ULI

Z MLG TFROGB EVIWRXG

NO SUCH LUCK

Well-loved barfly Iain Cooper died this evening at Oonagh's Irish Pub after he came in to celebrate a winning million-dollar lottery ticket. Foul play was suspected since Iain was killed by his well-known allergic reaction to peanuts, despite the fact that Oonagh's doesn't carry any nuts or peanut-based ingredients. And although multiple witnesses stated Iain brought his winning ticket into the bar with him, it wasn't on his body after his death. Investigators questioned three suspects the following day: Quinn, the bartender working the night before; Duffy, a friend of Iain's and a regular face at Oonagh's; and Liam, a comic who sometimes hosted open mics at the pub. When asked about the last interaction they had with Iain, the witnesses gave the statements below:

QUINN: Iain was the kindest soul you ever met. He ordered a bottle of Irish whiskey for every table in the bar last night, said that it was the only way to truly celebrate. He even took a bottle for himself, but it was sealed when I gave it to him, so I don't know how he ended up with peanuts in his system.

DUFFY: Iain and I were always arguing about which Irish whiskey was the best and that night was no different, but we only ever fought in jest. Especially when he was sharing bottles of the finest with us all. I was happy for the guy. And it didn't hurt that I knew he'd be sharing his payday with his friends. He was just that kinda guy. I played a round of very poorly aimed darts with him before I went home for the night, but he looked happy and healthy as a clam when I left.

LIAM: I didn't actually know the guy that well. I come into the pub to crack a few jokes and make a few bucks, and I'm out. He seemed nice enough though. He even let me take a swig of his bottle of GlenDronach before I took off for the night. Shame to lose the guy.

After reviewing the witness statements, detectives were able to determine that one of the suspects had lied in their statement and brought them in for further questioning. Which witness was lying, and how did the detectives know?

ONE WAY OUT

You've chased a criminal into one of the most confusing and spiraling neighborhoods you've ever seen, filled with dead-end cul-de-sacs and even a few one-way streets. There's only one way out of this neighborhood, and the thief you're after knows it. Can you find the right way out, while obeying any one-way streets you come across?

ABOVE SUSPICION

Detective Mason's recent flight home to visit family turned chaotic after a passenger was found dead halfway through the flight and a bottle of poison was discovered on the floor near the deceased's seat. While he was unable to run prints on the bottle during the flight, Detective Mason believes his interviews with the passengers on the flight will give him everything he needs to crack the case.

Only three people on the plane had enough access to the deceased (who sat in a middle seat) to be able to poison him during the flight: the flight attendant, the deceased's childhood best friend, and a woman named Alicia.

The passenger who sat in the window seat, to the left of the deceased, happened to be the mother of the dead man's ex-girlfriend, and neither she nor Maura had anything nice to say about the man.

Sita asked the flight attendant if she could change seats as soon as she boarded the plane—requesting to move to the aisle seat just to the right of the soon-to-be dead man.

Two of the three suspects both witnessed the third suspect (who happened to be the daughter of someone the dead man had recently fired) slip poison into the victim's drink.

Who were the three primary suspects, how did they have access to the deceased, what relationship did the suspects have to the dead man, and who was the guilty party?

A PICTURE-PERFECT CRIME

A precocious art student noticed that some of the paintings at the Mallory Rock Art Museum are near-perfect forgeries. Since the galleries have CCTV cameras running nonstop, the forgeries must have replaced the originals sometime before the paintings were hung on the walls. The museum manager Kate Svitko pointed the police to her number one suspect: Travis Reilly, a museum security guard who confessed to lying about having a criminal past. Reilly swears he's innocent, but in the alley behind the museum, the police found a coded message and a partially smudged key. Can you determine if this clue will convict or clear Reilly's name?

(coded message in symbols)

◁• = T	V = R	∧ = Y	# = L
□ = D	⬱ = C	ℕ = M	⊕ = P

DANGEROUS ANIMALS

The police suspect a local pet shop is being used as a front for laundering money. The police don't have enough for a warrant, but during an undercover visit to the shop you spotted a scribbled note behind the counter that at first glance looks like nonsense. Luckily you snapped a photo to study later, but can you crack the message to break open the case?

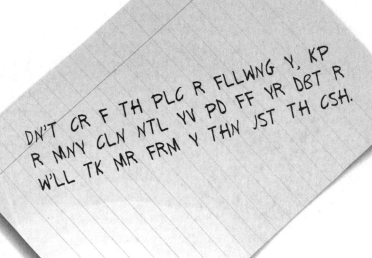

DN'T CR F TH PLC R FLLWNG Y, KP
R MNY CLN NTL YV PD FF YR DBT R
W'LL TK MR FRM Y THN JST TH CSH.

RUNNING IN THE FAMILY

Two sisters have been accused of breaking into Blackwell Prison to help their two brothers escape, but the sisters say even if they wanted to, there's no way it could possibly have been done. The prison is surrounded by a moat, and spotlights illuminate all areas of the water nonstop. A small boat was discovered at the exterior edge of the moat near a forest, and after testing, showed it would have been able to carry at max capacity two of the sisters or one brother at a time.

There was a 55-minute window the night of the breakout in which one of the spotlights covering the moat was broken. But there was only one set of oars to row with, so each trip across the moat would have taken 7 minutes for one of the sisters to row, or 5 minutes for one of the brothers. Starting with both sisters near the forest on the exterior side of the moat, could the siblings have found a way to orchestrate this escape in the time allotted?

MY SISTER'S KEEPER

Harry Radcliff has been murdered and every member of his family is a suspect. Detectives tried interviewing the widow Erin and her three adult children, Camille, Kat, and Cory separately, but Erin has kept the family lawyer close at hand to keep everyone in the family quiet. After the family members left the station, Detective Jacobs was sure he'd hit a wall in the case. That is, until he noticed a note left behind by Camille, scribbled onto a fast food wrapper she left behind. On its own, it looked like just a series of random letters, but by tracing a path between the letters and only using each letter once, he thinks he might find a lead for his case. Can you unravel the mysterious maze of letters?

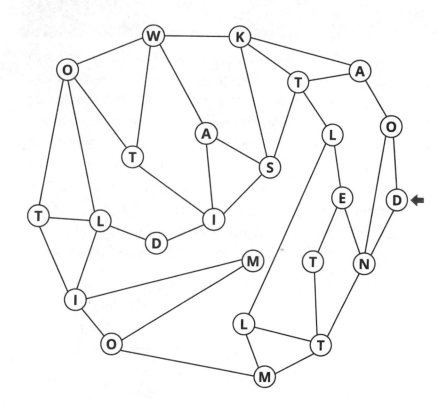

YOU CAN'T TAKE IT WITH YOU

The funeral for the late Morganna Mead erupted into chaos this morning after Morganna's daughter noticed five bejeweled rings were missing from her mother's hands inside her casket. After interviewing every mourner in attendance, the police focused their questioning on the last three people to approach Morganna's casket before her daughter was told the priceless rings were missing. The witnesses in question were: Davina, Morganna's childhood best friend; Pauline, Morganna's sister; and Gino, Morganna's estranged son. Their statements, as collected by police, are as follows:

DAVINA: The rings were on my dear friend's hands when I paid my respects. Pauline was in line right behind me, and I saw Gino approach the casket after Pauline. I don't know why anyone's upset though. Everyone knows Morganna had the gemstones replaced with fakes years ago.

PAULINE: I paid my respects just before Davina and the rings were still on Morganna's hands then. I was surprised to see them though, since Morganna had promised the rings to my five daughters.

GINO: I know my sister doesn't trust me, but I'm the one who told her the rings were missing. I saw Pauline pay her respects at my mother's casket, followed by Davina, and I went to say my goodbye's after Davina. But when I got there, I noticed my mother's cherished rings were gone and went straight to tell my sister.

After reviewing the witness statements, detectives were able to determine that one of the suspects had lied in their statement and brought them in for further questioning. Which witness was lying, and how did the detectives know?

ESCAPE INTO A GOOD BOOK

There's been a prison break, and the guards have been at a loss for how the prisoner escaped. The morning of the escape, the prisoner received a book in the mail, *Whose Body,* written by mystery writer Dorothy L. Sayers, that looked harmless at the time, but on closer inspection, has three long sentences highlighted and contains a bookmark with a series of numbers on it that had first been mistaken for dates. Could these be a clue to cracking how the criminal escaped?

If you have read my book on "Criminal Lunacy," you will remember that I wrote: "In the majority of cases, the criminal betrays himself by some abnormality attendant upon this pathological condition of the nervous tissues. His mental instability shows itself in various forms: an overweening vanity, leading him to brag of his achievement; a disproportionate sense of the importance of the offence, resulting from the hallucination of religion, and driving him to confession; egomania, producing the sense of horror or conviction of sin, and driving him to headlong flight without covering his tracks; a reckless confidence, resulting in the neglect of the most ordinary precautions, as in the case of Henry Wainwright, who left a boy in charge of the murdered woman's remains while he went to call a cab, or on the other hand, a nervous distrust of apperceptions in the past, causing him to revisit the scene of the crime to assure himself that all traces have been as safely removed as his own judgment knows them to be. I will not hesitate to assert that a perfectly sane man, not intimidated by religious or other delusions, could always render himself perfectly secure from detection, provided, that is, that the crime were sufficiently premeditated and that he were not pressed for time or thrown out in his calculations by purely fortuitous coincidence.

2/1/8, 2/2/2, 2/2/3, 4/4/1, 5/3/1, 6/3/6, 8/4/5, 9/1/4, 9/2/11, 10/1/3, 11/2/4, 11/3/4, 12/5/5, 13/1/1, 14/1/4, 14/4/1, 16/2/1, 18/1/5, 19/1/3, 20/3/5, 20/5/5, 21/1/1, 21/3/5, 22/1/7, 26/5/4, 29/1/1, 29/3/1, 33/5/4, 34/3/7, 37/3/5, 45/2/2

EXIT STAGE DEATH

Theater director Scott Connelly was found dead backstage just after the opening night of his stage adaptation of Arthur Conan Doyle's Sherlock Holmes story *The Adventure of the Mazarin Stone*. The murder must have taken place during the performance, so many of the actors would have been backstage, but each actor claims they saw nothing out of the ordinary. After searching the theater top to bottom, you find a program for the play with some odd notations and numbers on it. Can you decode the message and uncover the mystery behind this possible murder?

STARRING:

ABC

Ryan Christie as Sherlock Holmes	**Phil Gaddin** as Dr. Watson	**Ava Dennis** as Mrs. Hudson
Ricky Green as Billy the Page	**Davis LaRue** as Count Sylvius	**Wyatt Gentill** as Sam Merton
Joel Black as Lord Cantlemere	**Luke Vitalli** as Understudy #1	**Anna James** as Understudy #2

PG-1, JB-3, AJ-3
RG-1, LV-3, RG-2, RC-2
AJ-2, DL-2, RG-2
AJ-1, DL-2, JB-3, LV-3, AJ-2,
AJ-1, AJ-2, LV-3, AD-1, RC-2
AD-1, RC-1, AD-1,
PG-1, JB-3, AJ-3
DL-2, AD-1, RC-1, RG-2
AJ-2, JB-3
WG-2, DL-3, WG-3, WG-3
DL-2, DL-3, JB-1

STEALING THE SHOW

Detective Herring recently caught Kelly King, one of the most notorious thieves of all time. While being interrogated, King bragged about a few of her favorite thefts, three of which had not previously been connected to her.

One of the stolen items was the Graff Hallucination Watch, another item has an estimated worth of 20 million dollars, and the third item King gave to her sister as a gift before her sister left town. King lost the stolen item worth $55 million in a poker game last week.

The Messiah Stradivarius violin that King stole was crafted in 1716 by Antonio Stradivari, and despite being a highly coveted item, is worth less than the 1962 Ferrari GTO she stole.

Only one of the three stolen items is still sitting at King's Malibu property and able to be returned to its owner, but it's not the item worth $48 million.

What items did Kelly King steal, how much was each item worth, and where are the items now? And which of the three items can still be recovered and returned to its owner?

AKA

Detective Sophie Horne has gone undercover more than any other officer in her precinct, recently infiltrating a drug ring, a pharmaceutical company, a multilevel marketing company (MLM), a religious cult, and a prison. She used different aliases for each undercover assignment (Sian Shore, Callie Cole, Meg Moreau, Lianna Lawson, and Nikki North), and each time was looking for evidence regarding a different crime (grand larceny, murder, tax evasion, identity theft, and bribery). Use the following clues to piece together which group Horne infiltrated in what year, which alias Horne used to infiltrate which group, and which crime was being investigated at the time.

The assignment where Horne went by the name Meg Moreau happened before the undercover operation that had Horne infiltrating a prison and after the undercover operation that targeted a religious cult.

The operation that happened in 2023 involved a case of bribery, and did not include the use of the alias Lianna Lawson.

Horne went undercover for the identity theft case sometime before she went undercover for the murder case.

The first undercover assignment Horne ever had was infiltrating a pharmaceutical company. The undercover assignment that happened in 2024 did not involve a drug ring.

Between the religious cult and the case that involved identity theft, Horne used the alias of Callie Cole for one operation and Meg Moreau for the other.

Horne went undercover using the alias of Nikki North in either 2017 or 2019. Horne did not use the alias of Sian Shore when she targeted the MLM.

The five undercover assignments Horne completed are: the one that targeted an MLM, the case that involved tax evasion, the one where she used the Lianna Lawson alias, the one that occurred in 2019, and the one that targeted a drug ring.

		TARGET				
		Drug Ring	Pharma Co.	MLM	Cult	Prison
YEAR OF THE OPERATION	2017					
	2019					
	2021					
	2023					
	2024					
ALIAS	Sian Shore					
	Kate Cole					
	Meg Moreau					
	Lianna Lawson					
	Nikki North					
CRIME	Grand Larceny					
	Murder					
	Tax Evasion					
	Identity Theft					
	Bribery					

	CRIME					ALIAS				
	Grand Larceny	Murder	Tax Evasion	Identity Theft	Bribery	Sian Shore	Callie Cole	Meg Moreau	Lianna Lawson	Nikki North

LEAD
DETECTIVE

OIL AND WATER

When a ship carrying three guards and three prisoners arrested for grand larceny, forgery, and fraud starts to sink, the men on board figure they are done for. Neither the prisoners nor the guards could swim, and there is only one lifeboat on board that would allow them to escape to a nearby island, but it only seats a maximum of two people at a time. The guards must never be outnumbered by the prisoners, either on the ship or on the island. The lifeboat will be swept out to sea if there is not someone to man the motor. And while the prisoners are eager to escape, they would never try to do so without saving the lives of the guards first. They may be criminals, but these three would draw the line at murder.

Can you get all six men off of the sinking ship and safely to the island without the prisoners overtaking the guards?

COURTROOM CONSEQUENCES

After losing his case, David Moon, the defense lawyer handling the class action lawsuit against ABQ Pharmaceuticals, was found dead in his office Monday morning. He left a suicide note, but all his files were missing and the police think it might be a case of foul play, but they haven't been able to find any witnesses and the security cameras were broken hours before the time of death. The only other item found in Moon's desk was a bunch of letters scribbled on the last page of his notepad. Can you make heads or tails of it?

NS DN FW YM VS T VH CHC
YLN HT S HTD-FL YM SL
R SC HT NW T M DLT QB
F C HT

TAKEN A DARK TURN

After hours of chasing a murderer through a series of underground tunnels in the city, you've finally caught him —only to find yourself lost with four paths to choose from to get yourself and the dangerous captured killer out. Can you find the *shortest* way out of the tunnels? The longer you're down there, the more opportunities your captive will have to get the upper hand and leave you stranded in the dark!

ALL IN

In a wild twist of fate, Detective York has arrested five criminals on the same day, all at the legendary Pantheon Casino in Las Vegas. Each criminal (Alf, Brick, Grey, The Truck, and Bruiser), worked independently of the others, and each was arrested for a different crime (counterfeiting, extortion, murder, pick-pocketing, and tampering with the intent to cheat) and used a fake ID while in the casino (Gordy T., Josh B., Lisa F., Maria T., and Ravi R.). Using the clues below, figure out which criminals operated under which name, how much each was able to steal before their arrest, the time of their arrest, and the crime they were each charged with.

The first three digits of the amount of cash stolen by the criminal charged with extortion (whose fake ID did not say Maria T. or Lisa F.) match the digits of the time they were arrested.

If Grey (who did not go by the name Josh B.) had not been arrested, they would have walked away with an amount of money that would have been perfectly divisible by their family of three.

Brick, (AKA Ravi R.) did not murder, extort, or pick-pocket anyone.

The five arrested criminals were: The Truck, Josh B., the person who stole $130K, the counterfeiter, and the person arrested at 11:55 p.m.

Before they got caught for extortion, Bruiser had stolen 100 times more than Alf.

The criminal answering to the name of Gordy T. spent hours at the casino either swapping counterfeit chips with other players or pickpocketing. He was arrested last but accumulated the least amount of money.

The murderer (who stole $33K) was caught later than the person who tampered with the slot machines (who wasn't caught at 6:15 p.m.).

Between The Truck and the person going by Lisa F., one was a counterfeiter, and the other was caught at 8 p.m.

		NAME ON FAKE ID				
		Gordy T.	Josh B.	Lisa F.	Maria T.	Ravi R.
CRIMINAL	Alf					
	Brick					
	Grey					
	The Truck					
	Bruiser					
TIME OF ARREST	2:50 p.m.					
	4:00 p.m.					
	6:15 p.m.					
	8:00 p.m.					
	11:55 p.m.					
AMOUNT STOLEN	$130K					
	$2.5K					
	$9K					
	$33K					
	$250K					
CRIME	Counterfeiting					
	Extortion					
	Murder					
	Pick-Pocketing					
	Tampering					

	CRIME					AMOUNT STOLEN					TIME OF ARREST				
	Counterfeiting	Extortion	Murder	Pick-Pocketing	Tampering	$130K	$2.5K	$9K	$33K	$250K	2:50 p.m.	4:00 p.m.	6:15 p.m.	8:00 p.m.	11:55 p.m.

TO THE GRAVE

Infamous gossip columnist Mac Kanin was found dead in his apartment just hours after word got out that he was writing a memoir exposing a long covered-up scandal related to one of his friends or family members. Detective Norcott suspects that the person Mac was writing about must be the murderer, but despite getting into Mac's computer, a file folder labeled THE BOOK is password protected with a code that has so far eluded officers. Detective Norcott found a series of letters scribbled on a piece of paper taped underneath Mac's laptop but entering them as is for the password has not worked. On the keyboard itself, there is a backward arrow pointing at the letter M at the bottom of the keyboard. Using these clues, can you unravel the puzzle, unlock Mac Kanin's final work in progress, and get Detective Norcott one step closer to solving this case?

A GOOD NEIGHBOR

Angry and antagonistic neighborhood grouch Ferris Patrick died last night. His body was discovered this morning after a delivery person spotted him on the floor of his living room. While all of his neighbors claim not to have seen anything suspicious, Mr. Patrick's outdoor security cameras caught three people entering his house and then exiting it with a concealed item the morning after the murder. And while there were no cameras inside the home, Detective Lyons is determined to uncover if foul play was involved.

Of the three people caught on camera, neither Rose nor the suspect seen entering and exiting the house at 7 a.m. could stand Tracy because she was constantly shouting at Mr. Patrick over the state of his unkempt lawn.

Ed told the person who snuck out of Mr. Patrick's house with a rare first edition of Agatha Christie's *Nemesis* that he was surprised they hadn't bumped into one another, because he was in the house shortly after they left it at 6:45 a.m.

The person who snuck into the house at 8 a.m. took the opportunity to retrieve an item Mr. Patrick had borrowed from them months ago. Mr. Patrick never returned the item, claiming he lost it, but his death provided the perfect chance for the item to find its way home.

The neighbor who swears Mr. Patrick had been stealing his newspaper for the past 12 Sundays in a row did not leave the house with an old candlestick.

While one neighbor snuck into Mr. Patrick's to steal a priceless book and a second neighbor snuck in to retrieve their borrowed belongings that only had sentimental value, the person who snuck out of Mr. Patrick's house with a marble paperweight came back to the house to grab it after remembering they'd left their prints on the murder weapon.

Who were the three suspects, what time were they seen sneaking in and out of the house, what item did they sneak out of the house with, what did they fight with the victim about, and was there foul play involved? If so, who is the guilty party?

A MURDER ON 34TH STREET

A serial killer has struck fear into the heart of the small town of Hawk Springs, Wyoming. On Christmas Eve, three city council members were murdered in their homes, with a cryptic message left behind, pinned to each body with a knife: "MERRY CHRISTMAS," followed by a string of symbols. Can you decode the message and help detectives get one step closer to understanding this case?

MERRY CHRISTMAS

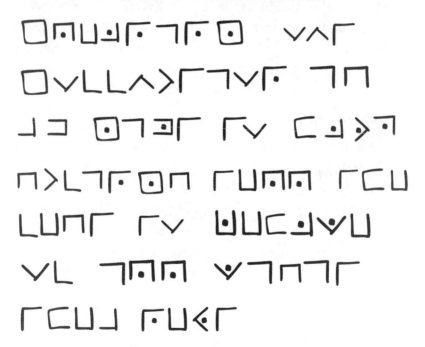

IN THE DARK

A recent earthquake knocked the power out last night throughout half of the city, including a complete blackout during a private gala at the brand-new Pantheon Museum. The prestige event required attendees to leave their phones at the coat check, so with the power out, everyone truly was in the dark. And when the lights returned, a priceless jadeite and black opal letter opener had disappeared from its display case. The lights were not out long enough for many of the museum's guests to reach the display in time to steal the eye-catching item, so detectives have prioritized getting statements from the three people closed-circuit TV showed were closest to the display just before the blackout: Romesh, the museum curator; Alan, a retired gemologist; and Fern, a recently retired museum guard. Their collected statements from the evening are as follows:

ROMESH: I was supposed to meet a date at the museum tonight but she never showed up. I wanted to show her that letter opener too. It's one of the most expensive items we've been able to get on loan for the museum's grand opening. I regretfully think we focused far too much on acquiring impressive items to show off at the gala, and perhaps not enough time vetting our guests and security system.

ALAN: I heard there were items on display this evening that haven't been seen by the public in person in decades! What a joke to get here and have the lights go out and not be able to see them at all, with one of 'em missing, and then to have the evening cut short. I got here late too so I only got to see a few items before I came into the room with the letter opener. By that time, most of the guests were in the main hall, but I remember, that museum curator was pretty close to that letter opener display, right before it went lights out.

FERN: I've seen a lot of great exhibits in my work, and last night's was one of the best. I arrived early and got to see each display before the lights went out. I didn't spend much time looking at that letter opener though. I'm not really a fan of jade. That's why I was more focused on the Hutton-Mdivani Necklace on the other side of the room when the lights went out.

After reviewing the witness statements, detectives were able to determine that one of the witnesses had lied in their statement and brought them in for further questioning. Which witness was lying, and how did the detectives know?

LAST WORDS

At the reading of the will for millionaire and world-renowned bank robber Jonathan Chen, his seven children and three ex-wives were shocked to learn that the deceased thief died with not a penny to his name. Instead, he left the following letter along with a passage from one of his favorite books: *Shuddering Castle* by Wilbur Fawley. He also privately left his only granddaughter Juliana a photobook filled with cherished photos. After some time, Juliana discovered a small key behind one of the photos and noticed a series of numbers scribbled on the back of each picture as well. She suspects this might be a clue to finding the money Jonathan had stolen over the years, and wanting to do the right thing, approached Detective O'Shannon and you for help solving her inherited mystery. Can you figure out the connection?

The numbers on the photos in the order they appear in the album:

2 / 5 / 2 / 1, 1 / 4 / 3 / 1, 6 / 1 / 7 / 1

2 / 4 / 10 / 1, 6 / 1 / 12 / 1, 2 / 4 / 15 / 1, 1 / 7 / 17 / 1

6 / 1 / 19 / 1, 3 / 1 / 2 / 2, 2 / 5 / 3 / 2

2 / 1 / 6 / 2, 5 / 4 / 7 / 2, 1 / 1 / 8 / 2

3 / 6 / 9 / 2, 3 / 2 / 12 / 2, 6 / 3 / 13 / 2, 5 / 1 / 15 / 2, 3 / 4 / 1 / 3, 2 / 1 / 2 / 3, 1 / 2 / 3 / 3

5 / 4 / 3 / 3, 2 / 3 / 4 / 3, 8 / 1 / 6 / 3, 6 / 2 / 6 / 3

4 / 3 / 7 / 3, 4 / 4 / 7 / 3, 2 / 6 / 7 / 3, 3 / 4 / 8 / 3, 7 / 4 / 8 / 3

"When I was at school, I thought life was learned from books," he went on, warming up a bit. "Life—I love it. And life at its utmost, that's reporting. Life that ticks off love, laughter, tears on every second. A foundling left on a door-step. Strange disappearance of a college girl. She's never seen or heard of again. Mystery. Death by misadventure. Murder. Fire-traps. Tenement fire—father, mother and grown-up kids burned to a crisp. Pet poodle, whining, discloses the baby under a bed, unharmed. Baby is adopted by a rich family. Poodle gets a decoration. Stories! Stories!"

He drew a deep breath, and continued: "The great thrill is putting your story over, hot off the press, satisfying the public's curiosity for news. Exclusive stories! The first thing the City Editor looks for. But there's no credit for them outside the office force. A pat on the shoulder, 'Good work, Bill!' and sometimes a 'by-line.'

You write a good story, and you wallow in self-esteem. That's the only real compensation. No wallowing in wealth.

The tragedy of reporting is that newspaper stories pay so little and die so quickly. You put your life's blood into them, your very soul. But they're not even yesterday's remembrance. In a couple of days they're dead—dead as a pickled herring!"

To my insufferable children and former wives, I would not be surprised if you rejoiced at my passing or even intentionally caused it, but I take heart knowing there will be no inheritance for a single one of you. I can only hope my dearest grandchild Juliana can look backward to all the wonderful times we had before my passing, as those memories hold the greatest treasure of all. In life and in death, Jonathan.

BOTTOMS UP

William Bowler has gone missing. For the last three years, he's worked at Nicky's (B)arcade, but last Friday near the end of his shift, he collected a tip from a patron, retreated into the kitchen for his break, and was never seen again. A cook in the kitchen saw William crumple up a note he received with his tips and toss it in the trash before leaving the kitchen. The note consisted of an eight-sided stop sign with some letters on it, followed by a string of numbers, but he couldn't make heads or tails of it. Using the note on the following page, can you solve the mystery of the missing bartender?

1-3
4-2, 5-2, 1-4, 7-3
8-2, 1-4, 1-5
7-3, 1-3, 7-1, 5-2, 1-2,
6-3, 6-3
5-3, 6-2, 1-4, 7-1, 1-2,
2-2, 7-1, 1-3, 1-4, 5-2
1-3, 6-3
5-2, 1-4, 7-1
1-1, 6-3
3-2, 1-4, 1-4, 2-3
1-1, 6-3
1-3, 7-1
1-5, 6-3, 1-2, 2-3
7-1, 1-4
2-1, 1-2

AFRAID OF GETTING CAUGHT

Change just one letter on each line to go from the top word to the bottom word. Do not change the order of the letters. You must have a common English word at each step.

G U I L T Y

_____

_____

_____

_____

_____

_____

_____

_____

_____

S C A R E D

HOW TO KEEP A SECRET

Therapist Victor Schaefges was found shot to death in his office this morning, and investigators suspect the murder was committed by one of his patients last night around 9 p.m. Victor left notes in his patients' files if they ever had excessively angry outbursts in their sessions, and there were three such patients that investigators found most suspicious.

Of those three, one was an artist, another was the patient who says they were at the movies at the time of the murder, and the third was a patient named Jo, who was seeing Victor to deal with her anxiety issues.

The electrician who was out to dinner at the time of the murder and Al both had appointments with Victor the day of the murder.

Bea and the nurse were both newer patients, one of whom was seeing Victor for help dealing with their angry temper, while the other was seeing Victor to help them with the fallout after a scandalous affair.

Multiple witnesses were able to confirm the artist's alibi of working late in their studio at the time of the murder—something they did often after one of their notorious angry outbursts. But the killer's alibi fell apart after they mentioned seeing a movie at their local theater without realizing the theater had been closed this week for repairs.

Who were the three primary suspects, what were their occupations, what were their alibis, why were they seeing the therapist, and who was the guilty party?

CONS ABOUT TOWN

A number of con artists have been causing havoc in Washington, DC, by running scams throughout the city. Detectives Kreider and Vischer have determined that the con artists have scammed a total of five targets (journalist Emerson Hauge, senator Steve Viel, Luxury Gem's Jewelry Boutique, Legacy Realty, and the Pendersen Auction House). The criminals been working in teams of different sizes (one solo and others in teams of 2, 3, 4, and 5), with each job bringing in a different size score to be split among the schemers. Also, each crew or solo criminal left behind a taunting letter to the police that signed off using the name of their crew as a calling card. Causing a headache for all, a junior detective at the station accidentally mixed up the crew names in all of the case files. Use the clues noted by the detectives to correct the mistake and to determine which cons were committed against which businesses, as well as the amount of money pilfered and how many criminals had to split the stolen cash.

The Auction House (which was not targeted with the Melon Drop con) resulted in a score that amounted to $60K per member once it was split up. Blind Justice needed an even number of crew members for their con.

The Mustard Dip con (which took away the smallest amount of money but didn't have to be divided among multiple people) was successful in stealing a bribe off of a singular person and not a business of any kind.

The Senator (who wasn't targeted by the Red Rebels) was conned by a group of four that walked away with an amount of money higher than the total of the other four scores combined.

The Foxes (who ran the Melon Drop con) did not go after the Journalist, the Senator, or the Realty Company.

The Hammer ran the Mustard Dip con by herself and walked away with a tenth of the money that was made by the Foxes (who walked away with $5K each).

The Red Rebels ran a color-themed con that required two fewer team members than the Dark Stars needed for their Big Store con, but each member of the Dark Stars walked away with almost double compared to what each member of the Rebels made.

		# OF MEMBERS				
		1	2	3	4	5
NAME OF THE CREW	Blind Justice					
	The Foxes					
	The Dark Stars					
	The Hammer					
	Red Rebels					
TARGETS	Journalist					
	Auction House					
	Realty					
	Senator					
	Jewelry Boutique					
TYPE OF CON	Big Store					
	Green Goods					
	Melon Drop					
	Mustard Dip					
	Toledo Panic Button					
$ TO SPLIT	$1K					
	$10K					
	$100K					
	$300K					
	$500K					

S TO SPLIT					TYPE OF CON					TARGETS				
$1K	$10K	$100K	$300K	$500K	Big Store	Green Goods	Melon Drop	Mustard Dip	Toledo Panic Button	Journalist	Auction House	Realty	Senator	Jewelry Boutique

MIXED MESSAGES

A pharmacist was arrested after a coworker reported him for tampering with a prescription bottle he gave to one of his customers. The pharmacist had slipped a note into a bottle of opioids the woman had been prescribed after breaking her arm, and the snooping coworker luckily took a photo of the note with what looks like a coded message before it was passed along. Can you decipher the secret note and figure out what the pharmacist's plans were?

Since the first moment I saw you, on the morning of 3/25, I've known we were meant to be together. I feel all mixed up knowing there are obstacles to our love, but if you can unscramble it all and put things right, I know you'll see just how much you mean to me.

Yours, Henry

LDJU UXXN VGETDCQ DQS IN VDHSK MGZ HV DBQ DE FUDHGWSR.

DEATH BY THE LETTER

A murderer has hidden the bodies of his victims somewhere in the forest outside of town and provided detectives with a puzzle that, when solved, will lead them to the correct location, if the puzzle is laid on top of a map of the area in question. Detectives have narrowed the possible burial site as one of four locations—marked in black on the next page—and they know the correct solution to the puzzle will yield a full phrase message from the killer to detectives. Starting at the outlined "H" and moving up, down, left, right, forward, OR backward (but never diagonal), can you map out the correct phrase and thereby find the right path through the forest to find the bodies?

```
E C T I V R Z A F A S M Y O W S N M A C K O O L T N O D
T E D A E N O E B T E J R X B I D V R T E G N B N I Z E
H E O W T H U N V E H I T E L N O E T J P ■ T U O A S L
L L L H G I S I C W I N E T Y S O R S F Q H H E L P U L
O C D A S T E S D E F L G H E E M C A E A T A E D J M R
D U R S N O B A D T R E E S W R O N N L M H P S G V E N
E M T I E N S M F I N D S T R O N G A T E R K I Y T E S
T E C V A L O U S E Z Y B H A N G E S C B L O O D Q S O
I Q B E J U T E T T ■ D E I V E W A K U P E H R E D H T
R P O T M C Q L M U O A W G A C K Y I L E T S L A W A R
L N I H V A R Y E R L Y S H I O U T O F T I M E R E M A
S G L L O T H T H I T W A S D E R S J E E K O Z I D B P
L K I E X A E R W G H E Y I N D T P O D U L L E V O L J
O O E D R E A D T Y D I D F R S H P U G H R A N T O N I
C K D I P A D B U O U R T Y A N E O D E A T H A S K E C
U M A C H E G O R R V W U O T T M N L Y R W Q Y E F W A
S E R K A L C D S T N A L M D D I E V C O X G O U I N Y
I V A Z T E R I O T L P H E X A L W H J R T B M A T D O
G D R M I S M E G N E N D B I F O R E N R E C T P S O U
R I N E F I S H E O S T O Y G U B G S T S H U T A T H ■
A W J O U T ■ D T L A R J J P O Q E D I V A L M E O N T
```

A REUNION CUT SHORT

Celebrated science fiction author Greg Dorff has gone missing. He was last seen three nights ago at his twentieth high school reunion, where he got into shouting matches with three of his former classmates. Detectives questioned all three scrappy schoolmates: Renee, a former girlfriend of Greg's; Brock, a friend of Renee's and former classmate to Greg; and Lenny, former classmate and football teammate to Greg. They collected the following statements:

RENEE: Greg and I were always on-and-off-again in high school. We hadn't spoken in over a decade though when I saw him enter the reunion, drunk to high heaven and asking me to give him another chance. I told him I wasn't interested but that didn't stop him from following me around half the night. I finally told him to get lost, and he started yelling. Thank god Brock was there.

BROCK: I heard Greg shouting at Renee and stepped in to try to calm things down, but then he just started having a go at me. Said something about how he'd bought tickets to take Renee to see the movie *Memento* freshman year, but I asked her to go see it first. He took a swing at me but missed and fell over. I don't think I ever even talked to the guy in school once. What a trip.

LENNY: Listen, nobody liked the guy. We tried to keep the reunion info private but somehow he found out about it and showed up. He started yelling at me about how I still owed him $100 from a Superbowl bet we made senior year in 2004, when the Panthers played the Packers. I shoved his head in the punch bowl and walked away. Didn't see him again the rest of the night.

After reviewing the witness statements, detectives were able to determine that one of the suspects had lied in their statement and brought them in for further questioning. Which witness was lying, and how did the detectives know?

SOLUTIONS

ASPIRING SLEUTH: BEGINNER PUZZLES

THE DISAPPEARING DONATIONS, page 24

Solution: This is an abjad cipher. Father Morgan's text reads: DONATIONS IN SAFE. PASSCODE IS FIVE FOUR SEVEN NINE SIX TWO.

FOR RICHER OR POORER, page 25

Key: The first number references the line of text and the second number references the word in that line.

Solution: WE WILL BE GONE FOR FIVE DAYS. TAKE EVERYTHING.

BODY OF EVIDENCE, page 26

SUSPECT	MOTIVE	CONNECTION TO THE VICTIM
Phyllis	Money	Ex-Wife
Cecilia	Jealousy	Former Client
Mei-Ling	Revenge	Law Firm Partner
Camille	Protecting Secrets	Current Wife
Margo	Paranoid Delusions	Rival Attorney

SPARK OF DANGER, page 28

FIRE

DIRE

DARE

HARE

HARD

HERD

HEAD

DEAD

DON'T WAKE THE DEAD, page 29

Niles is lying. He mentions hearing music blasting from Richie's trailer at 7:45 p.m. but Maggie gave Richie headphones around 7:40 p.m. and Bruce confirmed Richie had been quiet that evening, since Goat Midwinter sent a thank you for keeping the noise down.

THICKER THAN WATER, page 31

Key: In the body of the email, the alphabet is shifted 10 places to the right, so A = K, B = L, C = M, and so on. The separation of the word *ten* in the subject line is a clue.

Solution: I DID THIS FOR YOUR OWN GOOD, LUCY. I WON'T LET HIM HURT YOU AGAIN.

PAINT BY MURDER, page 32

If West takes the painting first, Blake will kill Vine. If West takes Blake first, Vine will destroy the painting. So West must take Vine first to the patrol car and lock him in the back. Returning to the studio, West could take the painting to the car, and return with Vine. Then leave Vine in the studio and take Blake to the car to sit with the painting until West retrieves Vine and brings him down last.

Or, once Vine is in the patrol car, West could take Blake to the car, and swap Blake into the car, taking Vine with him back to the studio. Then leave Vine in the studio while he takes the painting down to the car, leaving the painting safely with Blake, while returning to the studio one last time to retrieve Vine and bring him down to the car last.

Takes seven moves.

FAMILY TIES, page 33

Key: The letters on a phone keypad start on the number 2, which leads to the correct grid and answer. In each number combination, the first number represents the number on the phone keypad and the second number represents the letter on that phone keypad number.

Solution: AND WIPE YOUR PRINTS OFF MY KEYCARD WHEN YOURE DONE. XO MOM

LIES IN THE LIBRARY, page 34

Alex is lying. He says Victoria was using the Good Fences app on the computer in question, but Noel and Victoria corroborate that she was writing in her notebook and stayed for less than half the time Alex mentions.

TAKE THE MONEY AND RUN, page 36

Answer: 27 - 81 - 28 - 14 - 98

OUT OF LINE, page 38

The order of the lineup from left to right: Pete, Tommy, Carver, Benny, Cord, and Redd. Benny was in position four; therefore, he was positively ID'd as the suspect.

DON'T LET HIM FIND YOU, page 39

L I S T E N

LISTED

LILTED

TILTED

TILLED

TILLER

K I L L E R

'TIL WHOSE DEATH DO WE PART, page 40

Key: The alphabet is reversed.

Solution: THE MARRIAGE IS JUST FOR MONEY JACK. I LOVE YOU.

THE HONORABLE DETECTIVES, page 42

DETECTIVE	CAREER-MAKING CASE	YEAR THEY JOINED THE FORCE
Campos	Arson	2011
Blake	Bank Robbery	2009
Orsen	Murder	2010
Franklin	Narcotics	2012
Torres	Cybercrime	2013

A MOROSE CODE, page 44

Key: The message is written in Morse Code.

A	· —	H	· · · ·	O	— — —	V	· · · —
B	— · · ·	I	· ·	P	· — — ·	W	· — —
C	— · — ·	J	· — — —	Q	— — · —	X	— · · —
D	— · ·	K	— · —	R	· — ·	Y	— · — —
E	·	L	· — · ·	S	· · ·	Z	— — · ·
F	· · — ·	M	— —	T	—		
G	— — ·	N	— ·	U	· · —		

Solution: IVE PAID MY DEBT TO THE BANK

RISING STARS, page 45

Harold was the youngest. He caught the Ponzi schemer at age 25. Conner caught the political blackmailer when he was 26. Logan caught the tax evader when he was 27.

PICK YOUR POISON, page 46

Button #1 will free you.

PRIVATE INVESTIGATOR: INTERMEDIATE PUZZLES

M.I.A. OR R.I.P.?, page 50

Key: This is a date shift cipher. Use the date in the email subject, and the subject "ODDS & EVENS" to surmise that the odd words have shifted by the first number in the date cipher: 2, and the even words in the message have shifted by the second number in the date cipher: 19.

	A	B	C	D	E	F	G	H	I	J	K	L	M
	N	O	P	Q	R	S	T	U	V	W	X	Y	Z
(2)	C	D	E	F	G	H	I	J	K	L	M	N	O
	P	Q	R	S	T	U	V	W	X	Y	Z	A	B
(19)	T	U	V	W	X	Y	Z	A	B	C	D	E	F
	G	H	I	J	K	L	M	N	O	P	Q	R	S

Solution: DROP OUT OF THE ELECTION AND DISAPPEAR OR WE RELEASE THE VIDEO.

BAD BLOOD, page 51

The sister was killed by the husband, who was killed by the nephew, who was killed by the granddaughter, who was killed by the son, who was killed by the sister.

RELATIONSHIP	OCCUPATION	WEAPON	ORDER OF DEATH
Sister	Mayor	Gun	1
Son	English Teacher	Car	5
Nephew	Tattoo Artist	Poison	3
Husband	News Anchor	Pillow	2
Granddaughter	Bartender	Peanuts	4

THE VERDICT ON THE VERDICT, page 54

Key: This is an atbash cipher, so the alphabet is reversed.

Solution: FIFTY THOUSAND FOR A NOT GUILTY VERDICT

NO SUCH LUCK, page 55

Liam is lying. Quinn and Duffy both confirmed Iain had bought bottles of Irish whiskey for the room and himself but Liam mentions drinking Iain's bottle of GlenDronach, which is a Scotch whisky, not Irish.

ONE WAY OUT, page 57

ABOVE SUSPICION, page 58

Alicia sat in the window seat to the left of the victim. She was the mother of the man's ex-girlfriend. Sita sat in the aisle seat to the right of the victim. She was childhood best friends with the dead man. Maura was the flight attendant who waited on the victim and the daughter of an employee recently fired by the man. She was also the killer.

You can create a logic grid puzzle to organize the information provided. The first three clues give you the information you need to create the grid, and the fourth clue allows you to find the guilty party using the now-created grid.

	Alicia	Maura	Sita	Childhood Best Friend	Mother of Ex-Girlfriend	Daughter of Fired Employee
Flight Attendant	X	O	X	X	X	O
Window Seat	O	X	X	X	O	X
Aisle Seat	X	X	O	O	X	X
Childhood Best Friend	X	X	O			
Mother of Ex-Girfriend	O	X	X			
Daughter of Fired Employee	X	O	X			

A PICTURE-PERFECT CRIME, page 59

Key:

● = A   ⬖ = B   ⬗ = C   ▢ = D   ▣ = E

⬛ = F   ⟩ = G   ∞ = H   ⚌ = I   ✳ = K

♯ = L   ∾ = M   ◉ = N   ✕ = O   ⊕ = P

∨ = R   ⊖ = S   ◁ = T   ✛ = U   ∧ = Y

First, decode the letters using the key. To fill in the rest of the message, try decoding the one-letter word with either an A or an I. Since I _ D doesn't make a lot of sense for the second three-letter word in the puzzle, we can assume the single-dot symbol represents an A. Using that in the second three-letter word in the message also lets us assume that word is most likely AND.

Solution: THANKS FOR YOUR HELP KATE AND CONGRATS ON BECOMING A MILLIONAIRE LYDIA

DANGEROUS ANIMALS, page 60

Key: All of the vowels are missing from the note.

Solution: I DON'T CARE IF THE POLICE ARE FOLLOWING YOU, KEEP OUR MONEY CLEAN UNTIL YOUVE PAID OFF YOUR DEBT OR WE'LL TAKE MORE FROM YOU THAN JUST THE CASH

RUNNING IN THE FAMILY, page 61

Sister 2 stays near the forest while Sister 1 crosses to the prison.

Sister 1 stays at the prison while Brother 1 crosses to the forest.

Sister 2 returns the boat to the prison and picks up Sister 1.

Both sisters return to the forest edge, and Sister 1 stays with Brother 1.

Sister 2 returns to the prison and stays.

Brother 2 takes the boat alone, crossing to the forest, and stays with Brother 1.

Sister 1 takes the boat back to the prison.

Sister 1 picks up Sister 2 and both return to the edge of the forest.

Takes eight moves and 52 minutes.

MY SISTER'S KEEPER, page 62

Solution: DON'T TELL MOM I TOLD IT WAS KAT

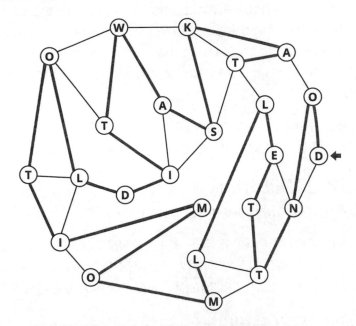

YOU CAN'T TAKE IT WITH YOU, page 64

Davina is lying. She says she paid her respects before Pauline and Gino, but both Pauline and Gino say Pauline was the first out of the three of them to pay their respects.

ESCAPE INTO A GOOD BOOK, page 66

Key: The first number in each date represents the line, the second number represents the word, and the third number represents the letter.

Solution: LUNCH DUTY SIDE DOOR UNLOCKED NOON GO

EXIT STAGE DEATH, page 68

Key: The coded message uses the initials of the actors in place of the numbers in a keypad cipher, and the ABC scribbled in the top right corner of the program's grid of the cast lets you know the initials will pair with the letters on a phone keypad, just like a normal keypad but shifted one box to the right.

Solution: YOU DREW THE SHORT STRAW AVA, YOU HAVE TO KILL HIM

STEALING THE SHOW, page 70

The stolen Graff Hallucination Watch was worth $55 million, and King lost it in a poker game.

The stolen 1962 Ferrari GTO was worth $48 million, and King gifted it to her sister.

The stolen Messiah Stradivarius violin was worth $20 million and is sitting in King's home. It's the only item that can currently be recovered and returned.

AKA (ELIMINATION/LOGIC GRIDS), page 71

YEAR	TARGET	CRIME	ALIAS
2017	Pharma Co	Tax Evasion	Nikki North
2019	Cult	Grand Larceny	Callie Cole
2021	MLM	Identity Theft	Meg Moreau
2023	Drug Ring	Bribery	Sian Short
2024	Prison	Murder	Lianna Lawson

LEAD DETECTIVE: ADVANCED PUZZLES

OIL AND WATER, page 76

One prisoner and one guard cross. The prisoner exits the lifeboat, onto the island.

The guard returns and exits the lifeboat onto the burning ship.

Two prisoners cross and drop off one prisoner on the island.

One prisoner returns to the ship and exits the lifeboat.

Two guards cross. One guard is dropped off on the island, and one prisoner gets on the lifeboat.

One guard returns to the ship with that one prisoner. The prisoner gets back on the ship.

A second guard joins the guard still on the lifeboat. Both cross to the island, exiting onto the island.

The guards send one prisoner in the lifeboat alone back to the ship.

The prisoner picks up a second prisoner at the ship, returns to the island, dropping that prisoner off.

One prisoner returns to the ship one last time and picks up the last prisoner.

The final two prisoners cross to the island and complete their escape from the sinking ship.

Takes 11 moves.

COURTROOM CONSEQUENCES, page 77

Key: This message is written backward so first you must reverse the letters to get:

TH C F BQ TLD M T WN TH CS R LS MY LF—DTH S TH NLY CHC HV T SV MY WF ND SN. Then add the missing vowels back in.

Solution: THE CEO OF ABQ TOLD ME TO WIN THE CASE OR LOSE MY LIFE. DEATH IS THE ONLY CHOICE I HAVE TO SAVE MY WIFE AND SON.

TAKEN A DARK TURN, page 78

ALL IN, page 80

CRIMINAL	TIME ARRESTED	FAKE ID	CRIMINAL CHARGE	$ STOLEN
Alf	11:55 p.m.	Gordy T.	Pickpocketing	2.5K
Brick	4:00 p.m.	Ravi R.	Tampering with intent to cheat	130K
Grey	6:15 p.m.	Lisa F.	Counterfeiting	9K
The Truck	8:00 p.m.	Maria T.	Murder	33K
Bruiser	2:50 p.m.	Josh B.	Extortion	250K

TO THE GRAVE, page 84

Key: Start with the QWERTY alphabet, as arranged on a keyboard from left to right, top to bottom. Then reverse that alphabet back to front to decode the message and get the password for Mac's computer.

Solution: MY SECRET WEAPON

A GOOD NEIGHBOR, page 85

Tracy snuck in and out of Mr. Patrick's house the earliest, at 6:45 a.m., to grab the rare first edition of Agatha Christie's *Nemesis*. Tracy's fights with Mr. Patrick were about his unkempt lawn.

Ed was in and out of the house second, at 7 a.m. He came to grab the marble paperweight because it had his fingerprints on it and it was used as the murder weapon the night before, by him. Ed's fights with the deceased were about Mr. Patrick stealing his newspaper.

Rose snuck in and out of Mr. Patrick's house latest, at 8 a.m. She came by to retrieve a candlestick she had lent to Mr. Patrick that he claimed to have lost. They fought over the missing item.

A MURDER ON 34TH STREET, page 87

Answer Key:

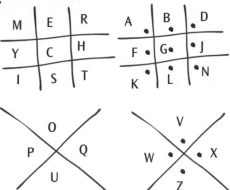

The coded message uses a combination of a keyword cipher and a pigpen cipher. Use the letters in MERRY CHRISTMAS as a shift cipher for the pigpen cipher.

Solution: Cleaning out corruption is my gift to Hawk Springs. Tell the rest to behave or I'll visit them next.

IN THE DARK, page 88

Fern is lying. She says she hates jade, but the Hutton-Mdivani Necklace is also made of jade.

LAST WORDS, page 90

Key: First, you must work backward on each set of numbers, clued in by the fact that the first number in the set of four would have to stand for the paragraph number, and there are only three paragraphs in play. Then, the first number represents the paragraph, the second number represents the line, the third number represents the word, and the fourth number represents the letter, which gives you this message: OWTEVIFENOXOBTISOPEDKNABSYERG. Finally, reverse this message.

Solution: GREYS BANK DEPOSIT BOX ONE FIVE TWO

BOTTOMS UP, page 92

In the vein of a keypad cipher, the stop sign has "aieou" at the top. If we assign those letters 1-1, 1-2, 1-3, 1-4, and 1-5, there are 7 more sides to the sign and 21 more letters, so 3 consonants can be placed alphabetically (minus the vowels) along each side, going clockwise from the top. So, BCD are 2-1, 2-2, and 2-3. And FGH are 3-1, 3-2, and 3-3, and so on.

Solution: I KNOW YOU. WITNESS PROTECTION IS NOT AS GOOD AS IT USED TO BE.

AFRAID OF GETTING CAUGHT, page 94

GUILTY

GUILTS

GUILES

GUIDES

GLIDES

SLIDES

SLICES

SPICES

SPACES

SPARES

SCARES

SCARED

HOW TO KEEP A SECRET, page 95

Al, a nurse, was seeing the therapist to deal with his scandalous affair and said he was at the movies at the time of the murder.

Bea, an artist, was seeing the therapist for anger issues and was at work at the time of the murder.

Jo, an electrician, was seeing the therapist to deal with her anxiety and was out to dinner at the time of the murder.

Al was the killer, since his alibi of being at the movies didn't hold up.

CONS ABOUT TOWN, page 96

CREW	#	CON	TARGET	SSS
Hammer	1	Mustard Dip	Journalist	$1K
Foxes	2	Melon Drop	Jewelry Boutique	$10K
Red Rebels	3	Green Goods	Realty	$100K
Blind Justice	4	Toledo Panic Button	Senator	$500K
Dark Stars	5	Big Store	Auction House	$300K

MIXED MESSAGES, page 100

Key: Using the date provided in the message to decode the date cipher, every other letter will be shifted accordingly. The first letter—and all odd letters—are shifted by 3, and all even letters shifted by 25.

	A	B	C	D	E	F	G	H	I	J	K	L	M
	N	O	P	Q	R	S	T	U	V	W	X	Y	Z
(3)	D	E	F	G	H	I	J	K	L	M	N	O	P
	Q	R	S	T	U	V	W	X	Y	Z	A	B	C
(25)	Z	A	B	C	D	E	F	G	H	I	J	K	L
	M	N	O	P	Q	R	S	T	U	V	W	X	Y

This gives you the message: IEGV RYUO SHBUADN ENT FO SEETH NDA EW ACN EB GREEHTTO. Then unscramble each word.

Solution: GIVE YOUR HUSBAND TEN OF THESE AND WE CAN BE TOGETHER.

DEATH BY THE LETTER, page 102

HELLO DETECTIVE, THINGS LOOK DARK AHEAD BUT YOU DID FIND THE ONLY CORRECT PATH.

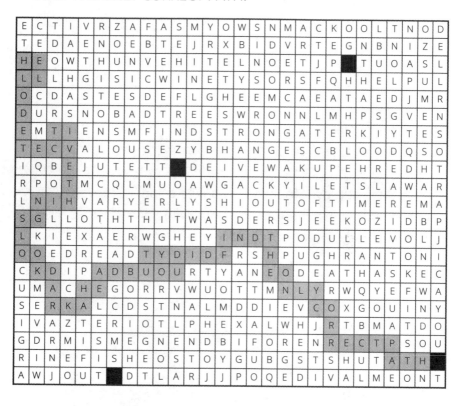

A REUNION CUT SHORT, page 104

Lenny is lying. He says he made a bet with Greg over the Superbowl in 2004 and mentions the Panthers playing the Packers, but the Panthers played the Patriots in 2004.

ABOUT HUNT◆KILLER.

Since 2016, Hunt A Killer has disrupted conventional forms of storytelling by delivering physical items, documents, and puzzles to tell immersive stories that bring friends and families together. What started as an in-person event has now grown into a thriving entertainment company with over 100,000 subscribers and over four million boxes shipped. Hunt A Killer creates shared experiences and community for those seeking unique ways to socialize and challenge themselves.